I0824926

"There is no book so bad...
that it does not have something good in it."

– Miguel de Cervantes, *Don Quixote*

MOPPET BOOKS

www.moppetbookspublishing.com

KinderGuides™ Early Learning Guides to Culture Classics
Published by Moppet Books
Los Angeles, California



ISBN: 978-1-7337921-2-7

Art direction and book design by Melissa Medina
Written by Fredrik Colting and Melissa Medina

*Special thanks to:*
Melody Foster, Jeannine Medina and Manny Medina

Printed in China

**Kinder**Guides

EARLY LEARNING GUIDE TO **MIGUEL DE CERVANTES'**

# DON QUIXOTE

*By* FREDRIK COLTING and MELISSA MEDINA

*Illustrations by* JOSÉ VILLAMAYOR

# Table *of* Contents

# About *the* Author

## MIGUEL DE CERVANTES

Miguel de Cervantes was a Spanish writer way back in time. He was born in 1547, and many people rank him as the greatest Spanish language author that ever lived. If people read your books hundreds of years after you're gone, that must mean you were really great!

His most famous book, *Don Quixote*, has been translated into over 140 languages and is the most-translated book in the world, after the Bible. Cervantes not only *wrote* books about adventures, he also experienced them himself. When he was a soldier in the Spanish Navy, he was captured by Turkish pirates and held as a prisoner for five long years. He tried to escape four times but was unsuccessful. Finally, his parents were able to pay his ransom and he returned to Madrid. Not long after that he wrote *Don Quixote*, which many scholars consider to be one of the best books ever written.

Alonso Quijano is a small-town nobleman living in the Spanish village of La Mancha with his niece and housekeeper. He has a very vivid imagination and his favorite hobby is to read books about brave knights and their tales of chivalry. In fact, he loves reading these stories so much that they become his obsession! So one day, he dresses up in an old suit of armor and decides that he is a knight himself, named Don Quixote.

Believing that he is a knight, Don Quixote decides to go out into the world to seek adventure and defend the helpless. Like all great knights, he needs a lady in whose honor he will serve. He chooses a poor peasant woman named Dulcinea, but because his imagination is getting the better of him, he is convinced that she is a princess.

So our delusional hero gets on his noble steed named Rocinante, who is actually just a tired old horse, and rides out to look for an adventure.

It's not long before Don Quixote arrives at a little tavern. However, because he's not seeing things as they really are anymore, he thinks it's a grand castle. He causes a lot of trouble and demands that the waiter, who he thinks is the lord of the castle, dub him a knight.

Eventually, Don Quixote rides on and encounters a group of travelers, and for some reason he thinks that they have insulted Dulcinea. He attacks them to defend her honor but only gets beaten up himself.

While Don Quixote is recovering at home, the housekeeper and a priest burn most of his books in the hopes that he'll stop believing that he is a knight. When Don Quixote wakes up, they tell him that a wizard did it. It's not very nice to lie, but they are trying to help him from getting into any more trouble.

However, Don Quixote seems to attract trouble. As soon as he feels better, he asks his neighbor, Sancho Panza, to be his page and ride the roads of Spain with him in search of glory and grand adventure. Sancho is a poor and simple farmer, but he agrees to go because Don Quixote promises to make Sancho a wealthy governor of his own town.

It doesn't take long before they run into trouble. When they come across a field of windmills, Don Quixote's imagination again gets the better of him. He believes the windmills are ferocious giants and sets off on Rocinante to attack them with his lance. He crashes into the windmills, breaks his lance in two and is knocked off Rocinante!

Sancho helps his master up and soon they are back on the road again. But it seems Don Quixote has still not learned his lesson.

They next encounter a group of friars that are accompanying a lady in a carriage. Don Quixote immediately thinks the friars are holding the lady captive, and he attacks them.

The fight ends with the lady telling the friars to pretend to surrender to Don Quixote so he will let them all go.

Feeling good about his latest victory, Don Quixote, followed by Sancho, ride on to a nearby inn. Once again, Don Quixote imagines that the inn is a castle and because he can't tell fact from fiction it leads to another fight. They both get hurt and try to cure their wounds with a special mixture Don Quixote calls The Balm of Fierabras. It tastes awful, and it makes them feel even worse!

When it's time to leave the inn Don Quixote refuses to pay their bill because he believes that all knights should stay for free. After all, they are working hard to save people. But so far Don Quixote hasn't saved anyone. In fact, he has been the one starting all the fights!

The manager gets so upset about the unpaid bill that he wraps Sancho in a blanket and tosses him out in the street!

Sancho is worried about his master and thinks he has had enough adventures. He calls on Quixote's friends, the priest and the barber, to come and convince him to come home. But Don Quixote refuses. Only when a police officer arrives to arrest him for starting all those fights does he let himself be locked in a cage and taken home—and only because they tell him it's a magic cage!

Back home, Don Quixote stubbornly refuses to believe he is not a knight. Sancho tries to get his master to think of something else besides knights and tells him that a wizard has transformed Dulcinea from a princess to an ordinary peasant girl. But the plan backfires and Don Quixote immediately makes it his mission to undo this magical spell and find the real Dulcinea!

Don Quixote is led to believe that if he fights a giant named Malambruno he will be able to save Dulcinea. So he and Sancho set out again, but this time on a wooden horse named Clavileño the Swift, that Don Quixote believes is a flying horse!

However, someone was storing fireworks inside the wooden horse's belly which suddenly explode, sending Don Quixote and Sancho flying through the garden!

Sancho, and everyone around him, have just about had it with Don Quixote's wild fantasies. But Don Quixote has a never-ending thirst for new adventures and talks Sancho into following him again. This time they set out to Barcelona where they happen to encounter a *real* knight, The Knight of the White Moon. Of course, Don Quixote challenges the Knight to a duel and the two begin to fight.

It's no surprise that the Knight of the White Moon is a much better knight (because he is a real knight), and he beats Don Quixote. The rules are that the winner gets to tell the loser what to do, so the Knight of the White Moon orders Don Quixote to lay down his armor and stop being a knight for one year.

Don Quixote finally realizes that his vivid imagination has caused a lot of trouble. He returns home to his village and announces his plan to stop being a knight. He even throws away all his knight equipment. He suddenly feels very old and writes a will that gives everything he owns to his niece, but only if she promises to marry a man that doesn't read books about knights. Don Quixote doesn't want her husband to go crazy like he did!

# Main Characters

## DON QUIXOTE

is the name that small-town Spanish nobleman, Alonso Quijano, gives to himself once he starts believing that he is a knight. Don Quixote is brave and chivalrous, but his headstrong thirst for adventure gets him into a lot of trouble.

## SANCHO PANZA

is a simple farmer hired by Don Quixote to join him on his adventures. He is the one that most often has to bail Don Quixote out of trouble.

## DULCINEA

is a poor peasant woman whom Don Quixote thinks is a beautiful and virtuous princess. She represents all that Don Quixote thinks is good and worth fighting for.

## THE PRIEST

is Don Quixote's friend who tries to get him to come back to reality.

## THE KNIGHT OF THE WHITE MOON

is a real knight that beats Don Quixote in a battle and makes him promise to not pretend to be a knight for a whole year.

# Key Words

## KNIGHT

A knight is a type of European warrior from hundreds of years ago that wore a suit of armor and was really good at fighting while riding a horse.

## OBSESSION

An obsession is something you do or think about so much that you can't think about or do anything else.

## DELUSIONAL

Being delusional is when you have a strong belief or vision of something that isn't really true or really there. Don Quixote experienced many delusions in this book.

## WINDMILL

A windmill is a structure with big blades or sails that uses wind energy to grind grain. Don Quixote famously picks a fight with the windmills because he thinks they are giants.

## HONOR

A person's honor is their good name and reputation. Medieval knights would often vow to defend or serve a lady's honor, just like Don Quixote vowed to serve Dulcinea's.

## LANCE

A lance is a long pole weapon used by knights to fight from horseback. Don Quixote uses one to attack the windmills.

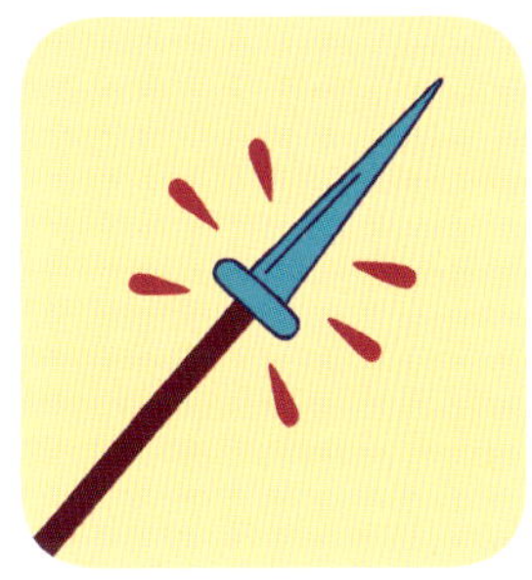

## LOYALTY

When you stick with what you believe in, or stick with someone else because of what they believe in, no matter what, you are loyal.

## DUEL

When two people had an argument a long time ago they sometimes settled it through a duel, which basically means that they fought each other until there was a winner.

# Quiz Questions

**Why does Don Quixote think he is a knight?**

A. He saw too many adventure movies

B. He read too many books about knights

C. His friend told him he was one

**What is the name of Don Quixote's horse?**

A. Spot

B. Cappuccino

C. Rocinante

**Why does Don Quixote attack the windmills?**

A. He thinks they are giants

B. He just hates windmills

C. He read it in a book

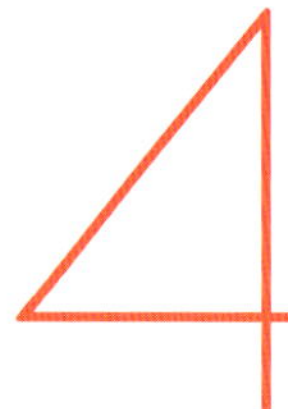

**What is the name of Don Quixote's adventure partner?**

A. Pancha la Mancha

B. Sancho Panza

C. Steve the donkey rider

5. **Don Quixote believes that Dulcinea is what?**

A. A knight

B. His niece

C. A princess

6. **How does the priest try to help Don Quixote?**

A. By burning his books about knights

B. By praying for him

C. By helping him with his armor

7. **How does the wooden horse fly?**

A. Don Quixote is imagining it

B. It's filled with exploding fireworks

C. It's a magic horse

8. **Who finally convinces Don Quixote to stop being a knight?**

A. The Knight of the White Moon

B. The Knight of the Blue Ocean

C. The Princess in the tall tower

ANSWER KEY 1: B / 2: C / 3: A / 4: B / 5: C / 6: A / 7: B / 8: A

# Analysis

*Don Quixote* by Miguel de Cervantes is considered one of the greatest books ever written and some call it the "first modern novel." This is because when it was released more than 400 years ago, nobody had read anything like it before.

In the story we follow Don Quixote, an older Spanish nobleman, who is obsessed with reading books about medieval knights who ride around saving beautiful women and slaying dragons and such. After a while, his vivid imagination takes over and he starts to believe that HE is a knight and that his mission in life is to go out into the world to have adventures and save those in need of saving. Of course, as we learn from the story, Don Quixote mostly tries to help people that don't really need helping and often creates chaos in the process. Luckily, he meets good-natured Sancho, who agrees to go on his adventures with him and helps him get out of trouble.

You can call *Don Quixote* a comedy because in many ways it's a very funny story. The way Don Quixote sees things that aren't there and believes that things like windmills are actually giants gives us a good laugh. In fact, there are many characters in the book that make fun of Don Quixote's madness (which is not very nice). But the truth is that the author's goal was not really to make fun of Don Quixote; he was actually making fun of the popular style of writing of his time, which was all romantic stories of medieval knights going on epic quests and falling in love. Cervantes thought it would be more interesting if his character WANTED to be like that, but wasn't really. And he was right. *Don Quixote* became more memorable than any other book from that time, and has influenced tons of other books, plays, music and movies. In fact, the word "quixotic" was coined in many languages after this novel to refer to a person who lets their imagination run away with them.